THE LORD OF THE RINGS

THE FELLOWSHIP OF THE RING

Photo Guide

Collins

An imprint of HarperCollinsPublishers

The Ruling Ring was made deep in the fires of Mount Doom by Sauron, the Dark Lord. Its magic can never be used for good, only evil.

"Sauron himself forged the One Ring. The molten gold was mixed with his own blood..."

Sauron loses the Ring in battle but he cannot rest until it is found...

His net spreads wide and he discovers that it is now in the hands of a hobbit called Bilbo Baggins, who lives with his nephew, Frodo, at Bag End in Hobbiton in the Shire.

"Smoke rises once more from the Mountain of Doom: the Shadow takes shape in the darkness of Mordor."

Frodo Baggins: *"Far too eager and curious for a hobbit."*

Few of the peoples of Middle-earth know much about hobbits. They live in holes and mostly keep themselves to themselves. But Frodo and Bilbo are different. They have always taken any chance to visit the world outside the Shire.

"Hobbits really are amazing creatures. You can learn all that there is to know about their ways in a month, and yet, after a hundred years, they can still surprise you…"

Bilbo Baggins: *"He's up to something, I'm sure of it."*

Most hobbits are wary of Bilbo's friend, Gandalf the wizard. He has a strange knack of turning up when something very important is about to happen.

"A wizard is never late, Frodo Baggins, nor is he early. He arrives precisely when he is meant to."

"Half the Shire's been invited and the rest of them are turning up anyway."

The Shire is buzzing with tales of mad Bilbo Baggins and the preparations for his most amazing birthday party.

Little does Frodo suspect that this party is going to change both their lives for ever…

"They are one, the Ring and the Dark Lord. Frodo, he must never find it!"

Gandalf the wizard tells Frodo about the Ring. Bilbo has left the Shire and Frodo is now the new Ring-bearer. But how can one hobbit hope to keep the Ring from all the forces of Sauron?

"Through me, it would wield a power too great and terrible to imagine. Do not tempt me, Frodo."

"The Ring is yours now…
Keep it secret, keep it safe."

*"Mr Frodo's not going anywhere
without me!"*

Sam is the youngest son of Old
Gaffer Gamgee, the gardener at Bag
End, and as sensible a young hobbit as
any in the Shire. He is fiercely loyal to
Frodo.

*"If I take one more step, it'll be the
farthest from home I've ever been."*

"You need people of intelligence for this sort of mission... quest... thing."

"Well, that rules you out, Pip."

Merry (Meriadoc Brandybuck), and Pippin (Peregrin Took) guess that their cousin, Frodo, is planning an adventure and they are determined not to be left behind...

*"It's a dangerous business going
out of your door... You step on to the road and
if you don't keep your feet, there's no knowing
where you might be swept off to."*

The Ring can only be destroyed in the fires of Mount Doom, in Mordor. Frodo sets out with Pippin, Merry and Sam on his long mission, knowing that he will be marked by every evil servant of Sauron.

"That Black Rider was looking for something... or someone..."

Gandalf the Grey is a member of the *Istari* – the Order of Wizards – who have been sent to help Middle-earth in their time of need. He is Frodo's friend and guide, although Frodo does not realise quite how powerful he is.

Saruman the White is senior even to Gandalf. He watches the world from the tower of Orthanc. Leaving Frodo behind, Gandalf travels alone to tell Saruman about the Ring, but learns he is not to be trusted.

"The world has changed, Gandalf.
A new Age is at hand..."

"Sauron's only measure is desire for power...
and so he will not think that, having the Ring, we may seek to destroy it."

Saruman has his own army, created from some of the most hideous life-forms in Middle-earth.

"By foul craft he has crossed orcs with goblin men."

"And now… perfected. Grown beyond the height of men – straight-limbed and strong, fearing nothing."

Leaving the Shire, the hobbits reach The Prancing Pony inn at Bree, hoping to find Gandalf the wizard. Instead, they find a tall, stern man who claims to be their friend. He warns them that they are in desperate danger from the Ringwraiths, the terrible Black Riders of Sauron.

"He's one of them Rangers, dangerous folk they are. Wandering the wilds. What his right name is I've never heard; but he's known round here as Strider."

Strider's true name is Aragorn and he is more than he seems… He is heir to the throne of Gondor.

"You are Isildur s heir, not Isildur himself. You are not bound to his fate."

"I must take you on paths few dare to tread."

"They were Kings... great Kings of Men.
Sauron gave to them Nine Rings of Power.
They took the Rings... and one by one, regardless
of their strength to good or evil... they fell."

Strider tells the hobbits to follow him to Rivendell, the home of Elrond Half-elven. They are in terrible danger, but at their darkest moment the elven princess Arwen, Elrond's daughter, arrives to rescue them…

*"Ride hard –
don't look back."*

"The road is too dangerous."

At Rivendell, Elrond calls a council of all the free people of Middle-earth, to decide how to destroy the Ring. Frodo is not to carry the Ring alone. There will be Nine Companions to stand against the Nine Servants of Sauron.

"Rivendell will soon become an island under siege. The Ring cannot stay here."

"The Ring was made in the fires of Mount Doom...
Only there can it be unmade."

With his double-headed battle-axe, Gimli is a great orc-killer and eager to join the Companions.

*"Gimli, Glóin's son...
known him since he was
knee-high to a hobbit."*

Legolas, the elf, has many special powers: his eyesight is sharper than an eagle's and his aim is deadly. Gimli and Legolas are so different, they are bound to clash. But both are united in their desire to see the Ring destroyed.

"Thranduil of the Woodland Realm has sent his son, Legolas."

"The Ring must be destroyed."

"There is weakness – there is frailty – but there is courage also, and honour, to be found in men."

Proud and ambitious, Boromir is a man from the ancient Kingdom of Gondor. He carries with him a great horn, tipped with silver, which he has only to blow for help to arrive.

But the test he faces may be too hard, even if the whole of Gondor comes to his rescue.

"Why not use the Ring?"

"It is a strange fate that we suffer so much fear and doubt over so small a thing."

"Nine Companions to match the Nine Ringwraiths... So be it."

"I will take the Ring to Mordor."

"We're coming too! You'll have to send us home tied up in a sack to stop us!"

"You have my bow..."

"And my axe."

*"If by my life or death,
I can protect you, I will.
You have my sword."*

*"I will help you bear
this burden, Frodo."*

*"You carry the fate of
us all, little one."*

The Fellowship of the Ring

It is time for the Nine Companions to leave Rivendell and set out on their mission.

Bilbo gives Frodo two of his own treasures: his sword, Sting, and a shirt of chainmail made from *mithril*, which is light as a feather and as hard as diamond.

"Sting was made by the elves. The blade glows blue when orcs are close."

"May the blessing of elves and men and all free folk go with you."

"The road goes ever on and on
Down from the door where it began.
Now far ahead the road has gone
And I must follow, if I can."

Always aware of the danger from the spies of Sauron, the Companions struggle upwards on the treacherous paths through the Misty Mountains. As they continue, snow falls and the road becomes impassable.

"It is not the strength of the body that matters,
but the strength of the spirit."

andalf knows of a secret way under the mountains, through the fabled Kingdom of Moria. But how will they find the password to let them through the Gateway?

"Dwarf doors are invisible when closed. Their own masters cannot find them if their secret is forgotten."

"Ithildin – it mirrors only starlight and moonlight."

"Moria – greatest of the dwarf halls."

"I fear the dwarves of Moria may have delved too deep."

Almost unimaginable terrors lurk beneath the mountain, and the old Mines of Moria have been overrun by the powers of darkness. Even as they try to escape from this underground tomb, the orcs are massing for attack...

"Be on your guard... there are older and fouler things than orcs in the deep places of the world."

"Here lies Balin, son of Fundin, Lord of Moria."

The Fellowship pays a terrible price for their escape from Moria. Pursued by orcs, they stumble on towards the elven kingdom of Lothlórien.

Orcs: *"They were once elves. Taken by the dark powers, tortured, mutilated – a ruined and terrible form of life, bred into a slave race."*

"I have heard tell of the strange magic of the Golden Wood..."

Orcs cannot overrun Lothlórien, the realm of Lord Celeborn and Galadriel, Lady of Light. But the Companions dare not rest for long.

Galadriel takes Frodo to look into her mirror. There he sees fragments from his future…

"Even the smallest person can change the course of the future."

"What you see I cannot tell, for the mirror shows many things… things that were… things that are and some things that have not yet come to pass."

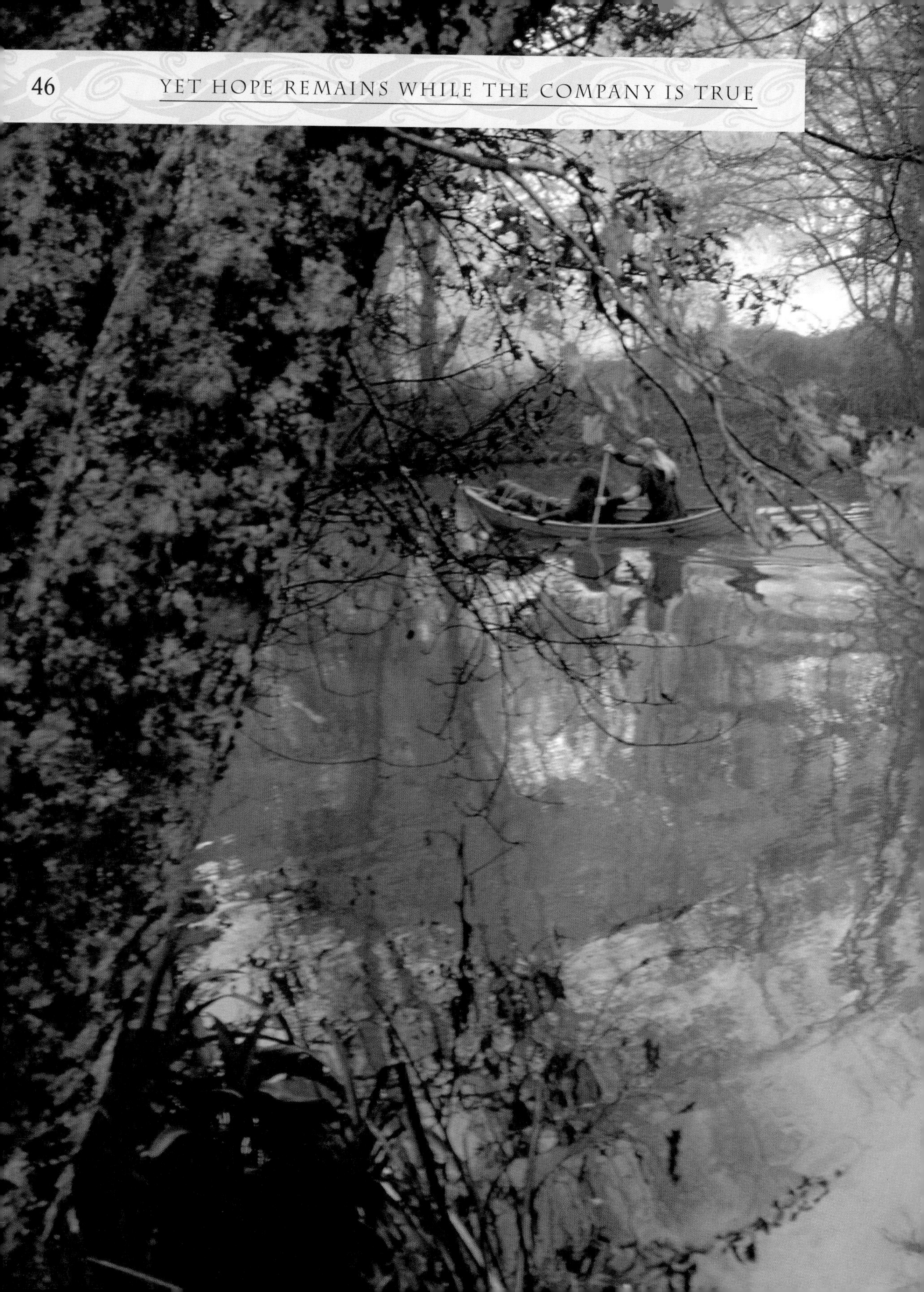

*"Somewhere in the world, a halfling
now wanders alone and unprotected,
bearing the Ring of Power."*